Touchpoints: The Power of Intimate Check-ins

Introduction

In the vast sea of human interactions, there exists a subset of encounters that deeply shape our relationships, lending them depth, meaning, and longevity. These are the touchpoints — the critical moments of connection that can turn ordinary relationships into extraordinary ones. They are the pauses in our often-busy lives, the times we intentionally choose to connect with another, delving deeper than the superficial layers. These touchpoints, in their quiet yet profound way, have the power to rejuvenate, reinvigorate, and reshape relationships. Yet, like many things that matter deeply, their value is often realized only in their absence.

The Role of Touchpoints in Strengthening Relationships:

Imagine walking on a sandy beach, each footstep you take leaves an imprint, momentarily capturing the essence of your presence before being washed away or blown over. Similarly, our lives, filled with myriad interactions and countless exchanges, leave impressions on others. Among these countless interactions, touchpoints stand out as the deeper imprints, those that withstand the tests of time and tide.

When we talk about relationships, it's easy to focus on the grand gestures—the anniversaries, the holidays, the celebrations, or the reconciliations after arguments. But in reality, the strength and depth of a relationship often lie in the ordinary moments made extraordinary by genuine connection. Touchpoints are these moments. They're not dictated by the calendar but by the heart. They are the quiet conversations in the middle of the night, the shared laughter over an inside joke, the mutual concern during challenging times, or the joy in celebrating each other's small victories. They're the times when we feel seen, heard, understood, and most importantly, loved.

A relationship without regular touchpoints is like a garden without water. It might survive for a while, but it can't truly thrive. The plants might look alright from a distance, but up close, the leaves are wilted and the roots are thirsty. Touchpoints, in the relationship landscape, are the nurturing rain showers and the rays of sunshine that invigorate and sustain our bonds. They ensure that relationships don't just survive but thrive, blossoming in full vibrancy.

Why Checking In Matters: Beyond the Surface:

In an age dominated by digital communications, the sheer volume of our interactions has exponentially increased. We're constantly in touch, but how often do we genuinely connect? There's a world of difference between a casual text message asking, "How are you?" and a heartfelt conversation where you dive into the depths of emotions, dreams, fears, and hopes. This is where the concept of 'checking in' gains paramount importance.

To check in is to intentionally pause, even if for a brief moment, to genuinely connect with another person. It's about moving beyond the veneer of everyday pleasantries and delving deeper. It's an invitation to share and to listen, to open up and to be present. When we check in, we're not just asking about someone's day; we're asking about their world.

Over time, these moments of sincere checking in accumulate. They act as the threads that weave the fabric of a robust relationship. They remind us that beyond the daily routines and the inevitable challenges, there's a bond that's worth cherishing. They are the touchpoints that keep the relationship anchored, ensuring that the bond, nurtured by mutual understanding and genuine care, remains strong and resilient.

Think about the relationships that have weathered the storms of life, the bonds that have withstood the test of time. Invariably, they have been punctuated with regular moments of checking in, of mutual understanding, of shared growth. These touchpoints, these check-ins, are what transform relationships from being mere associations to profound connections.

How to Make the Most of This Guide:

Embarking on the journey of deepening relationships through touchpoints is akin to setting sail on uncharted waters. It requires courage, commitment, and an open heart. This guide is designed as a beacon, shedding light on the importance of touchpoints, the magic of genuine check-ins, and the pathways to forge deeper connections.

To truly benefit from this guide, approach it with an open heart and an open mind. Recognize that while the concept of touchpoints might seem simple, its implementation requires sincerity. It's not about a checklist but about a mindset. It's about being present, being genuine, and being committed to the growth of your relationships.

As you journey through the pages, let each insight, each exercise, and each reflection be an invitation to connect more deeply. Remember, it's not about perfection but progression. There will be moments of profound connection and moments of missed opportunities. Embrace both with grace. Let the touchpoints be your guide, your compass, leading you towards relationships that are not just sustained but cherished, not just endured but enjoyed.

In the realm of relationships, the journey is as beautiful as the destination. And with touchpoints as your fellow travelers, you're set to embark on a journey filled with depth, meaning, love, and transformation. Embrace it, cherish it, and most importantly, live it.

Understanding Touchpoints

In the intricate dance of human interactions, there exists a myriad of fleeting exchanges and lingering connections. Among these, there are particular moments that hold a deeper resonance, like a single note that reverberates more potently in a symphony. These moments, characterized by genuine interest, concern, or shared joy, form the essence of what we term 'touchpoints'. Just as a single touch can send ripples across a still pond, these touchpoints send ripples across the landscape of our relationships, altering their nature and depth.

The Concept and Importance of Touchpoints:

At its core, a touchpoint is a significant moment of contact between two individuals, a moment that fosters deeper understanding and connection. It's more than a fleeting greeting or casual chat about the weather. Instead, it's an intentional pause, an opportunity to connect on a more profound level. In the context of relationships, touchpoints are the times when we truly see and are seen by another, where we hear and are heard, where we understand and are understood.

Life today often feels like a sprint, where we rush from one task to the next, one interaction to the next, without truly pausing. Amidst this hustle, the art of genuine connection is often lost. Touchpoints, in this landscape, emerge as the lifelines, anchoring us to the essence of human relationships. They are not mere exchanges of words but exchanges of feelings, emotions, and understanding.

Consider the most cherished memories in your relationships. More often than not, they are punctuated with touchpoints. They might be instances of shared laughter, mutual comfort during tough times, or times of pure, heartfelt conversation. These are the moments that elevate a relationship from being just another association to a cherished bond. They serve as reminders of the bond's depth and significance. In a way, touchpoints are the heartbeats of a relationship. They provide it with life, rhythm, and warmth.

Differentiating Daily Conversations from True Check-ins:

Conversations are an integral part of our daily lives. We engage in numerous discussions, ranging from casual banter to more serious deliberations. But it's crucial to differentiate between daily, routine conversations and genuine check-ins that qualify as touchpoints.

Daily conversations often revolve around the mundane and the routine. They can be about the weather, work updates, or casual greetings. While they serve a purpose in maintaining a basic level of connection and courtesy, they often lack depth. True check-ins, on the other hand, delve deeper. They are moments when one genuinely inquires about the other's well-being, not just physically but emotionally and mentally too. They are characterized by genuine interest, active listening, and a sincere desire to understand and connect.

A daily conversation might sound like, "How was your day?" followed by a brief, "It was good, thanks." A touchpoint or a true check-in, on the other hand, might involve probing deeper with questions like, "What was the highlight of your day?" or "You seem a bit off today, is everything okay?". It's the difference between skimming the surface and diving into the depths. While daily conversations maintain the continuity of a relationship, touchpoints enhance its quality.

The Science Behind Effective Check-ins:

Our understanding of touchpoints and their significance in relationships isn't just anecdotal. Scientific research, particularly in the fields of psychology and neuroscience, provides insights into why these moments of genuine connection hold so much power.

When we engage in sincere, heartfelt interactions, our brain releases oxytocin, often termed the 'love hormone' or 'bonding hormone'. This neurotransmitter plays a pivotal role in social bonding, trust, and building intimate connections. It's no surprise then that moments filled with genuine care, understanding, and empathy – the hallmarks of touchpoints – stimulate the release of oxytocin, thereby fostering bonding and trust.

Furthermore, genuine check-ins, characterized by active listening and empathy, activate the mirror neuron system in our brains. Mirror neurons are cells that fire both when we perform an action and when we see someone else perform that action. In the context of touchpoints, they help us "mirror" or resonate with another person's emotions and experiences, fostering understanding and empathy.

Lastly, from an evolutionary standpoint, humans, as social beings, have an innate need to connect, to belong, and to feel understood. Effective check-ins, or touchpoints, address this primal need. They assure us that we are valued, that we matter, and that we belong. In a world where feelings of isolation and disconnection are rampant, touchpoints serve as the bridges, connecting us to one another, reminding us of our shared humanity.

In wrapping up our exploration of touchpoints, it's essential to acknowledge that while the concept might sound simple, its implications are profound. It's not just about asking the right questions or saying the right things. It's about embodying a mindset, a mindset where relationships are not just endured but cherished, where connections are not just made but nurtured. It's about recognizing that in the grand theater of life, it's the genuine moments of connection, the touchpoints, that truly make a difference. Embracing them, therefore, is not just a choice but a commitment, a commitment to richer, deeper, and more fulfilling relationships.

Touchpoint 1. Self-awareness

The realm of relationships, diverse and intricate, often prompts individuals to journey inwards before stepping out to engage with others. This inward journey, a deep dive into one's psyche, beliefs, strengths, and vulnerabilities, becomes the compass guiding our interactions with the world. Self-awareness is not just an exercise in introspection; it's the beacon that illuminates our path in relationships, ensuring genuine understanding, empathy, and connection.

The role of self-understanding in relating to others is paramount. When an individual possesses a clear sense of self, they bring to the table authenticity, which becomes the bedrock of genuine connections. This doesn't mean having all the answers or being devoid of vulnerabilities. On the contrary, self-understanding implies recognizing and accepting our imperfections, celebrating our strengths, and having the humility to acknowledge areas of growth. By understanding ourselves, we can better predict our reactions, appreciate our needs, and set boundaries. This clarity paves the way for healthier interactions, ensuring that while we share our lives with others, we don't lose our essence in the process.

Relating authentically with others is an ever-evolving dance. It involves being present, listening actively, and responding with empathy. Yet, the efficacy of this dance is amplified when we truly understand the rhythm of our heart, the nuances of our mind, and the aspirations of our spirit. This understanding ensures that our interactions aren't just reflexive responses but are rooted in deep self-awareness. For instance, if someone is aware that they have a tendency to be defensive due to past experiences, this knowledge can help them pause, reflect, and respond more constructively in moments of disagreement.

Every individual, like a unique piece of art, is an amalgamation of strengths and weaknesses. Recognizing and embracing these aspects of ourselves is not just an exercise in self-acceptance but also a tool for building robust relationships. Awareness of one's strengths, be it empathy, resilience, patience, or any other virtue, enables an individual to contribute positively to a relationship. It allows them to offer support, understanding, and love from a place of genuine capability.

On the other hand, acknowledging one's weaknesses is equally vital. It's a humbling exercise, reminding us of our shared human frailty. By understanding our vulnerabilities, whether it's impatience, insecurity, or any other trait, we can communicate our needs better and work together with our partners, friends, or family to navigate these challenges. It's like understanding the weather patterns of one's internal landscape; while we can't always change the weather, knowing its patterns allows us to prepare, adapt, and grow.

Closely linked to the awareness of our strengths and weaknesses is the understanding of our triggers and emotional responses. Every individual, based on their life experiences, upbringing, and personal beliefs, has specific triggers—situations, words, or actions that evoke strong emotional responses. For some, it might be feeling unappreciated, for others, it could be the fear of abandonment, and for yet others, it might be the need for validation. These triggers, often rooted in past experiences, can manifest in the present, influencing our reactions, decisions, and relationships.

An exercise that aids in recognizing these triggers involves deep reflection. One could start by recounting instances where they felt a strong emotional upheaval. Understanding the situation, the people involved, and the exact emotion felt can provide insights into potential triggers. It's like joining the dots, where each emotional instance provides a clue to our deeper, often subconscious, triggers.

Along with understanding triggers, it's equally vital to recognize our emotional responses. Do we retreat into a shell when triggered, or do we lash out? Do we seek solace in solitude, or do we seek validation from others? By understanding our emotional patterns, we can consciously choose our reactions, ensuring they align with our values and contribute positively to our relationships.

It's crucial to remember that self-awareness is not a destination but a journey. As we grow, evolve, and gather more experiences, our understanding of ourselves will shift, expand, and deepen. Yet, at every point, this self-awareness will remain our trusted ally, guiding our steps in the vast world of relationships, ensuring that we relate with love, authenticity, and understanding. By turning inwards, we find the tools to step outwards with confidence, grace, and genuine connection.

Touchpoint 2. Communication

Human interactions, rich and varied as they are, often boil down to a symphony of words, gestures, and silences. Among the many threads that weave the fabric of relationships, communication stands out as both an art and a science. It's the bridge that connects souls, the language that translates emotions, and the tool that mends, builds, and sometimes, reshapes our bonds. As we delve into the intricacies of communication, it becomes evident that it's not just about speaking; it's as much about listening, understanding, and expressing with authenticity and clarity.

The art of listening is an oft-underestimated facet of communication. In a world brimming with voices, opinions, and clamors for attention, true listening has become a rare gift. Yet, it's a gift that has the power to transform relationships. Listening is not just about hearing words; it's about tuning in to the emotions, the unsaid, and the underlying currents. It's about being present, fully and wholeheartedly, with the person sharing their world with you. This kind of deep listening transcends mere auditory processing. It involves empathy, patience, and a genuine desire to understand another's perspective.

In any relationship, when one feels truly heard, it lays the foundation for trust and connection. It tells the other person that their feelings, thoughts, and experiences are valid and valuable. Imagine a friend sharing a concern, and instead of offering immediate solutions or changing the topic, you simply sit with them, offering your undivided attention, absorbing their words, and reflecting back understanding. Such moments are transformative, as they create a safe space for genuine expression and vulnerability.

Yet, while listening is half of the communication equation, the ability to express oneself clearly is equally crucial. Articulating our thoughts, feelings, and needs with clarity ensures that our messages are not lost in translation. It's not just about vocabulary or eloquence; it's about authenticity. Speaking from the heart, with sincerity, ensures that our words resonate with the listener. Every relationship thrives when individuals can express their joys, concerns, aspirations, and boundaries without fear of judgment or reprisal.

Clear expression also involves recognizing and managing our emotions. For instance, if one is feeling overwhelmed or frustrated, it's beneficial to acknowledge this emotion first, understand its root, and then communicate it in a manner that is constructive. This might mean taking a few moments to gather one's thoughts, choosing the right setting for the conversation, or even seeking the right words that truly encapsulate one's feelings.

For those seeking to hone their skills in listening and expressing, exercises can be invaluable.

The Two-minute Drill is one such tool. This exercise is straightforward yet powerful. It requires two participants. One person speaks about any topic of their choice for two minutes, while the other listens without interrupting. The listener's role is not to respond but to understand deeply. After the two minutes, roles are reversed. This exercise, when practiced regularly, hones the skills of both speaking succinctly and listening actively. Over time, participants often find that their attention spans improve, their ability to understand nuances is enhanced, and their capacity for empathy grows.

Another potent tool for improving communication is role-playing. Role-playing effective communication involves two participants assuming roles, often based on real-life situations or potential scenarios. These roles could be based on their experiences, or they might be entirely fictional. The aim is to navigate a conversation, understanding each other's perspectives, and arriving at a constructive outcome. For instance, one could assume the role of an individual seeking support from a friend, while the other could play the role of the friend. Through the conversation, both participants can explore various ways of expressing, responding, and understanding. Post the role-play, a discussion about what felt right, what could be improved, and the emotions experienced can provide deep insights into one's communication style and areas of growth.

The realm of communication, vast and profound, is an ongoing journey. As we navigate the pathways of relationships, the tools of listening and expressing become our trusted allies. They guide us, teach us, and often, uplift us. In every whispered secret, shared laughter, tearful confession, or earnest discussion, the magic of communication comes alive. It's the dance of souls, where words, silences, and gestures create a melody that resonates with the timeless desire for connection, understanding, and love.

Touchpoint 3. Building Trust

In the labyrinth of human connections, there's a singular thread that holds the entire structure together, preventing it from unraveling at the slightest tug of disagreement or misunderstanding. This thread, ethereal yet potent, is trust. Like the silent roots of a massive tree, trust anchors relationships, giving them the strength to weather storms and the nourishment to blossom. Exploring the dimensions of trust, its significance, and the ways to foster it can be the compass that guides us through the intricate map of human connections.

Trust, at its core, is the foundation of every strong relationship. It's the unspoken contract between friends, the bond between lovers, and the glue in families. When individuals trust each other, they build a safe haven, a space where they can be their authentic selves, voice their fears, share their dreams, and seek support. Trust is like a sanctuary where judgment is suspended, understanding is the primary language, and acceptance is the ambiance. It provides relationships the resilience to bounce back from conflicts, the elasticity to adapt, and the warmth of genuine connection.

The beauty of trust is its reciprocity. When one person trusts, it often inspires trust in return. It creates an environment of mutual respect, where vulnerabilities aren't exploited but are protected. In such a setting, every word spoken, every secret shared, and every gesture made adds another layer to the edifice of trust. But trust is not just a passive state of being; it's an active choice, a continuous effort. It's about keeping promises, showing up, being consistent, and sometimes, just being there, silent yet supportive.

However, building trust isn't always instinctive. It requires conscious effort, especially when past experiences might have left scars of betrayal or disappointment. Exercises designed to foster trust can be invaluable in such scenarios, offering individuals a structured pathway to rebuild and reinforce this vital element of relationships.

One such exercise is the Trust Falls. While many might be familiar with the basic concept, introducing variations can enhance its efficacy. The classic Trust Fall involves one person standing with their back to a partner, closing their eyes, and allowing themselves to fall backward, trusting the partner to catch them. This simple act, a leap of faith, encapsulates the essence of trust—letting go of control and believing in another's intent and capability. But variations can introduce new dynamics. For instance, introducing a gentle spin before falling can add an element of unpredictability. Another variation could be changing the setting, perhaps trying the exercise in a pool, where the water's buoyancy becomes an additional factor. Each variation offers a new perspective on trust, challenging participants to let go of apprehensions and embrace the essence of reliance.

Another exercise that delves deep into the realms of trust is Sharing Secrets. On the surface, it might seem like a simple act, but the ramifications are profound. Sharing a secret, especially one that has been closely guarded, is like handing over a piece of one's soul to another, hoping it will be cherished and protected. This exercise requires participants to exchange secrets, perhaps something they've never shared before. The act of sharing is just the beginning. The listener's response, whether it's empathetic silence, comforting words, or shared vulnerability, adds depth to the trust-building process. With time, as secrets are honored and protected, trust grows, solidifying its place in the relationship.

Navigating the nuances of trust-building, one realizes it's not just about grand gestures or profound revelations. Often, it's the everyday acts, the consistency in behavior, the gentle understanding, and the unwavering support that fortifies trust. It's the assurance that even in moments of doubt, disagreement, or distance, the foundation of trust remains unshaken.

In this dance of trust, as we twirl, leap, and sometimes stumble, we discover the profound joy of genuine connection. Trust teaches us to let go of our shields, to embrace vulnerability, and to find strength in mutual reliance. And as we walk the pathways of relationships, with trust as our guiding star, we experience the magic of unspoken bonds, the beauty of heartfelt confessions, and the warmth of hands that hold, not just in moments of joy, but especially in times of uncertainty. Trust, in its silent yet profound way, reminds us of the beauty of human connections, where hearts resonate, souls converge, and genuine love finds its true home.

Touchpoint 4. Navigating Conflict

The realm of relationships is vast and varied, painted with a spectrum of emotions that range from the purest joys to the most challenging adversities. Among these, conflict stands as an inevitable shadow, occasionally darkening the landscape of connections. While it might be tempting to view conflict as a disruptive force, it's more accurate to recognize it as an integral part of the relationship puzzle. Navigating through conflicts, understanding their roots, and employing strategies to resolve them can often transform these seemingly negative episodes into opportunities for growth, understanding, and deeper connection.

Understanding the source of conflicts requires an honest introspection into the dynamics of a relationship. Conflicts don't arise in isolation; they are often the result of underlying emotions, unmet needs, or unspoken expectations. For instance, a disagreement about spending habits in a partnership might not just be about money but could reflect deeper issues like security, control, or values. Recognizing these underlying themes is the first step in addressing the real issues at hand, rather than just the surface manifestations. By peeling back the layers of a conflict, we can arrive at its core, enabling a more holistic resolution.

But how does one navigate these layers without getting ensnared in the thorns of blame, resentment, or defensiveness? Here's where structured exercises can serve as guiding beacons, illuminating pathways through the often murky waters of disagreements.

The "No Blame" Game is an exercise designed to foster understanding without resorting to fault-finding. The premise is simple but profound. Partners or friends engage in a conversation about a contentious issue, but with one significant caveat: they consciously avoid placing blame on the other. This means phrasing sentences in a way that communicates feelings, needs, and perspectives without making the other person the antagonist. For example, instead of saying, "You never listen to me," the statement could be reframed as, "I feel unheard when we discuss this topic." This subtle shift changes the dynamics of the conversation. It creates a space where both parties can express their emotions without feeling attacked, paving the way for empathy and understanding.

Another invaluable tool in the conflict resolution toolkit is role-playing. Conflict Resolution Role-playing challenges individuals to step into the shoes of the other, allowing them to view the situation from a different lens. The exercise involves participants swapping roles and reenacting a disagreement. This reversal offers a unique perspective, enabling each person to understand the emotions, motivations, and concerns of the other. It's an exercise in empathy, a journey into the heart of another, which often reveals insights that might have remained hidden in the heat of the moment. After the role-play, a reflective conversation about the experience, the feelings elicited, and the new understandings gained can be incredibly enlightening.

However, while exercises provide structured pathways, the true essence of navigating conflict lies in the heart's willingness to understand, the mind's openness to perspectives, and the soul's commitment to the relationship. Conflict, in its inherent nature, shakes up the status quo, demanding attention and resolution. But this very disruption can be a catalyst for growth. When approached with a genuine desire to understand and resolve, conflicts can transform relationships, deepening the bonds, refining the dynamics, and introducing a level of intimacy that might have remained undiscovered in its absence.

Navigating conflict, in the end, is less about eliminating disagreements and more about harnessing their potential. It's about recognizing that every storm, no matter how fierce, eventually leads to clearer skies. It's about understanding that in the heart of conflict lies an opportunity: to grow, to understand, and to love more deeply. As we journey through the terrains of relationships, with their peaks of joy and valleys of disagreements, we learn the art of balance, the beauty of understanding, and the power of love that transcends all differences. In this dance of emotions, where conflicts and resolutions twirl around in an eternal embrace, we discover the true essence of relationships: a space where two souls converge, diverge, and always find their way back to each other, stronger, wiser, and infinitely more connected.

Touchpoint 5. Quality Time

Amid the cacophony of daily life, with its relentless routines and incessant demands, the essence of relationships often gets distilled into the moments of quality time shared between individuals. These moments, though sometimes fleeting, become the milestones upon which the journey of companionship is mapped. They are the anchors that ground relationships, providing both stability and sustenance. Delving into the depths of quality time, its significance, and the ways to cultivate it can enrich the tapestry of human connections, infusing them with vibrancy, intimacy, and enduring memories.

The value of shared experiences is multifaceted. On the surface, they provide immediate joy, a respite from the mundane, and a canvas for creating memories. However, diving deeper, one realizes that these shared moments are the threads that weave individuals together. Every shared laugh, every mutual discovery, and every collaborative challenge navigated adds another layer to the bond, solidifying the connection. Shared experiences become the reservoirs of memories, stories that can be revisited time and again, rekindling the emotions and reinforcing the bond. They serve as reminders of the journey traversed together, the challenges overcome, and the joys celebrated. More than just temporal diversions, these moments are the lifeblood of relationships, providing both context and continuity.

To celebrate the magic of shared experiences and to consciously cultivate them, certain exercises can be invaluable. The Memory Lane Walk is one such endeavor. It is a simple yet profound exercise that involves partners or friends revisiting places of significance in their relationship. It could be the café where they first met, the park where a crucial conversation unfolded, or any other locale imbued with memories. The act of physically revisiting these places serves as a portal, transporting individuals back in time, allowing them to relive the moments, savor the emotions, and reflect on the journey. It's not just about nostalgia; it's about recognizing the milestones, understanding the evolution of the relationship, and cherishing the shared path.

While revisiting the past has its charm, creating new memories is equally vital. The DIY Date/Activity Night serves this purpose. Instead of resorting to routine outings or activities, this exercise encourages individuals to craft their unique experience. It could be as simple as cooking a new recipe together, trying a DIY art project, or even setting up a backyard camping night. The emphasis is on collaboration, creativity, and novelty. Engaging in such self-designed activities not only provides an immediate sense of accomplishment and joy but also adds a unique memory to the relationship's repertoire, a moment that is distinctively "theirs".

In today's digital age, where screens often become the third entity in relationships, sometimes overshadowing real interactions, taking a deliberate break can be both challenging and rewarding. The 24-hour Disconnect exercise emphasizes just that. For a full day, participants commit to turning off phones, tablets, and other digital devices, immersing themselves entirely in the real world and, more importantly, in each other. This disconnection from the digital realm forces individuals to reconnect on a personal level, rediscovering the joy of undistracted conversations, the beauty of shared silences, and the magic of being truly present. It's a detox for the relationship, cleansing it of digital distractions and rejuvenating the connection.

Quality time, in its essence, is more than just the quantity of hours spent together; it's about the depth of connection achieved in those moments. It's about recognizing the impermanence of life and choosing to invest in moments that matter, with people who matter. As relationships evolve, navigating through seasons of change, challenges, and celebrations, it's the moments of quality time that serve as the beacons, illuminating the path, warming the heart, and reminding individuals of the beauty of shared existence. Through conscious efforts, like the exercises mentioned and an innate desire to connect, quality time can transform from being just intervals in a relationship to becoming its very core, pulsating with love, memories, and endless possibilities.

Touchpoint 6. Acts of Service

In the delicate dance of human relationships, words often take center stage, serenading the heart with sweet promises and earnest affirmations. But as enchanting as words can be, actions often speak louder, resonating deeply, echoing long after the words have faded. Acts of service, those deliberate endeavors to uplift, assist, or simply bring a smile, are powerful testaments of love, care, and commitment. They are tangible manifestations of intangible emotions, solidifying bonds and enriching connections. In this chapter, we embark on a journey to explore the profound impact of acts of service, understanding their significance and discovering ways to infuse them into our relationships.

Showing love and appreciation through actions has an age-old charm, rooted deeply in human nature. From the time of our ancestors, who would hunt and gather for their loved ones, to the modern-day gestures of making breakfast in bed or doing a favor unasked, service has been a language of love. It goes beyond the boundaries of verbal communication, addressing the more primal, fundamental aspects of care. Acts of service are direct responses to the needs and desires of loved ones, often even before they voice them out. They convey attentiveness, understanding, and a willingness to go the extra mile.

The beauty of acts of service lies in their versatility. They can be grand gestures, like planning a surprise trip or undertaking a significant task for someone. Yet, they can also be simple, everyday acts, like brewing a cup of coffee just the way a partner likes it or taking over a chore when the other is overwhelmed. Regardless of the scale, the underlying message remains consistent – I see you, I value you, and I'm here for you. This message, delivered through thoughtful actions, has the power to bridge gaps, heal wounds, and foster intimacy.

But how can one cultivate a mindset that naturally leans towards acts of service? Exercises, designed to stimulate such behaviors, can be instrumental. The Random Acts of Kindness Challenge is one such endeavor. Participants, be it partners, friends, or family members, commit to performing unexpected acts of kindness for each other over a specified period, say a week or a month. These acts can range from leaving sweet notes, preparing favorite meals, or even just setting up a warm bath after a tiring day. The unpredictability adds an element of surprise, making each gesture even more special. The challenge not only encourages individuals to think creatively about ways to make their loved ones feel cherished but also fosters an atmosphere of mutual appreciation and gratitude.

Taking the concept of service a step further is The Service Swap exercise. In this activity, individuals exchange a list of tasks or chores they usually handle. For a day or a week, they take over each other's responsibilities, stepping into each other's shoes. The exercise serves multiple purposes. First, it provides a break from routine, adding a novelty factor. Second, it fosters empathy, as individuals get a firsthand experience of the challenges and nuances of tasks they might not usually undertake. And third, it strengthens the bond, as both parties realize and appreciate the efforts the other puts into maintaining the relationship's equilibrium. The Service Swap is more than just an exchange of duties; it's an exchange of perspectives, understanding, and appreciation.

Acts of service, with their profound simplicity, have the potential to transform relationships. They cut through the noise, delivering clear messages of love, commitment, and care. In a world often dominated by words, where intentions can get lost in translation, actions stand tall, resonating deeply, touching the soul, and weaving bonds of trust, gratitude, and undying affection. They remind us that love isn't just about saying the right words but about doing the right things, consistently, selflessly, and wholeheartedly. Through acts of service, we transcend the superficialities, diving deep into the heart of relationships, where true connections are forged, cherished, and celebrated.

Touchpoint 7. Physical Connection

In the vast symphony of human connection, the notes of words, deeds, and thoughts combine harmoniously to produce a beautiful melody of love and affection. Yet, amidst these, there's a rhythm, a pulse, that often goes unsaid but deeply felt – the power of physical touch. As creatures of emotion and sensation, humans find comfort, solace, and pure joy in the embrace of a loved one, the touch of a comforting hand, or the synchrony of moving together. Physical connection, while seemingly straightforward, holds layers of emotional depth, offering myriad ways for two souls to communicate without uttering a word. This chapter unravels the beauty, necessity, and sheer joy of physical closeness in relationships.

The power of touch is ancient and profound. From the very moment we enter this world, we seek warmth, comfort, and security in the embrace of our caregivers. As we grow, this innate desire to connect physically only intensifies, molding itself to fit the myriad relationships we form. Touch becomes a language in itself, speaking volumes where words might fail. A comforting pat on the back, intertwined fingers, a spontaneous hug, or a gentle kiss on the forehead - each of these gestures carries messages of love, comfort, reassurance, and connection.

Physical closeness goes beyond just touch; it's about presence. It's the act of being there, fully and wholly, basking in the shared space and energy of a loved one. This proximity, this sharing of personal space, speaks of trust, vulnerability, and a mutual desire to be close. It's in these moments of closeness that barriers dissolve, masks fall away, and true connections are forged. The heartbeat becomes a lullaby, the warmth a blanket, and the touch a bridge, connecting two souls in a dance of love, trust, and intimacy.

Exploring and celebrating physical connection can be both a joyous and transformative journey. The Hug Challenge is a beautiful exercise to initiate this exploration. The premise is simple: participants challenge themselves to hug their partner, friend, or family member multiple times a day, making each embrace a bit longer than usual. While it might sound straightforward, the results are often profound. With each extended embrace, participants find themselves melting into the moment, letting go of external distractions, and simply being present. The heartbeats synchronize, breathing aligns, and a beautiful silence envelopes the two, making them realize the power and depth of non-verbal communication. This challenge isn't just about hugging; it's about understanding the comfort, love, security, and connection that such a simple act can offer.

Expanding the horizons of physical connection is the exercise Dance Together. Now, this isn't about perfect moves, synchronization, or rhythm.

It's about letting go, being in the moment, and celebrating each other's company without any judgments. Participants are encouraged to play their favorite tunes, or perhaps a song that holds significance in their relationship, and simply move. There's no right or wrong; it's all about expression. As the beats play and bodies move, participants often find themselves laughing, reminiscing, and connecting on a primal level. Dancing together breaks down walls, shuns inhibitions, and allows individuals to communicate in a language older than words - the language of movement, rhythm, and shared joy.

Physical connection, in all its forms, stands as a testament to the beauty of human relationships. It reminds us that while words and deeds have their place, there's an irreplaceable magic in just being close, in feeling the heartbeat of a loved one, in moving together to an unsaid tune, and in cherishing the sheer joy of touch. Through touch, presence, and shared movement, relationships find a depth that's both grounding and liberating. It's a journey back to the basics, to the core of human connection, where two souls find each other, lose themselves, and in that beautiful paradox, discover the essence of love.

Touchpoint 8. Words of Affirmation

In the intricate ballet of human relationships, actions frequently steal the spotlight, captivating audiences with their undeniable charm. Yet, lurking in the shadows, equally potent and enchanting, are words. These seemingly simple combinations of letters hold the power to heal, to comfort, to inspire, and to bind. Words of affirmation, those genuine expressions of appreciation, love, and support, play a pivotal role in nurturing and strengthening bonds. They serve as constant reminders of the beauty, depth, and significance of the connections we share. Dive deep with us into the ocean of verbal appreciation, and discover how these ripples of affirmation can create waves of happiness, understanding, and love.

The human soul, in all its complexity and depth, yearns for validation. At the core of our existence, there's a childlike desire to be seen, to be understood, and to be appreciated. Words of affirmation cater directly to this innate longing. They're not just compliments or casual observations; they're sincere recognitions of a person's worth, efforts, and essence. Verbal appreciation goes beyond mere flattery. It's a conscious acknowledgment of the qualities, efforts, and nuances that make a person unique. And when such affirmations come from loved ones, their impact is magnified manifold.

Every uttered word of love or praise is like a drop of nourishment for the relationship. It strengthens trust, bolsters self-esteem, and fosters a sense of security. When individuals feel appreciated and cherished for who they are, they naturally bloom, embracing their strengths, working on their weaknesses, and continually striving to be the best versions of themselves. Moreover, words of affirmation act as powerful tools to bridge misunderstandings, soothe wounds, and rekindle the spark in relationships. They're like the gentle rain that revives a withering plant, breathing life, love, and vibrancy into it.

But how does one cultivate a habit of verbal appreciation? How does one ensure that these words retain their sincerity and don't degrade into mere habitual utterances? Exercises focused on expressing affirmation can be instrumental in this journey. Consider the Compliment Jar. It's a heartfelt activity where partners, family members, or friends pen down genuine compliments for each other on slips of paper, collecting them in a designated jar. These can range from acknowledgments of physical attributes to deeper recognitions of character traits or actions. Over time, the jar becomes a treasure trove of love, appreciation, and fondness. On days filled with doubt, loneliness, or just the need for a boost, reaching into this jar and reading a compliment can work wonders. It's a constant reminder of the love and admiration that's present, even when unspoken.

Equally profound is the exercise titled Letters from the Heart. In an age dominated by digital communication, the charm of handwritten letters remains unparalleled. This exercise encourages individuals to write letters to each other, expressing their feelings, memories, hopes, and dreams. These aren't everyday notes but deep dives into the ocean of emotion. They can be letters of gratitude, reminiscing about shared moments, or heartfelt expressions of love and admiration. These letters become time capsules, capturing the essence of feelings at a particular moment, to be cherished, revisited, and celebrated in times to come.

Words, in all their simplicity, carry the weight of emotions, memories, and dreams. They're the threads that weave the fabric of relationships, binding individuals in bonds of love, trust, and mutual admiration. Words of affirmation remind us of the beauty of being seen, appreciated, and loved for who we are. They're the gentle whispers that reassure, the loud declarations that celebrate, and the silent promises that bind. Through sincere compliments and heartfelt letters, we not only express our feelings but also lay the foundations for deeper, more meaningful connections. After all, in the grand theater of life, words are the unsung heroes, silently scripting tales of love, understanding, and eternal connection.

Touchpoint 9. Building a Shared Future

In the dance of relationships, where two souls intertwine, the present holds its allure with the rush of emotions, the thrill of new experiences, and the comforting embrace of the known. However, as enthralling as the present might be, the future often holds a magnetic charm, beckoning us with the promise of shared dreams, aligned goals, and a life mapped together. Building a shared future is not merely about navigating the challenges of tomorrow, but it's about harmoniously blending two paths into one, ensuring each stride is taken in tandem, and every dream dreamt is one that resonates with both hearts.

As individuals, we each carry a repository of dreams, ambitions, and visions for the future. These dreams are often shaped by our past experiences, current desires, and hopes for what lies ahead. In relationships, the challenge and beauty lie in weaving these individual dreams into a shared tapestry of aspirations. It's about understanding, respecting, and, most importantly, aligning these visions to chart out a course that's fulfilling for both. This alignment doesn't necessarily imply sacrificing personal dreams for the sake of the partnership. Instead, it's about finding a harmonious balance, where both sets of dreams are acknowledged, discussed, and integrated into a shared vision of tomorrow.

The process of alignment begins with open, honest communication. It's essential for partners to lay bare their dreams, hopes, and fears for the future. This candid sharing creates a platform for understanding where each person sees themselves in the years to come, be it in terms of career, personal growth, family, or even geographical location. Such discussions can be enlightening, revealing synergies and differences, and laying the groundwork for compromise, adjustment, and mutual support.

Enter the Dream Board Session, a beautiful exercise designed to make these individual dreams tangible. In this activity, partners are encouraged to create visual representations of their aspirations, using pictures, quotes, symbols, and any other materials that resonate with them. These dream boards, created separately, serve as windows into each person's soul, showcasing what they truly yearn for. Once crafted, the boards are shared, and discussions ensue. The objective is not just to understand what each picture or symbol represents, but to delve deeper, exploring the emotions and stories behind them. It's an exercise in vulnerability and understanding, often leading to profound realizations about one's partner and oneself.

While the Dream Board Session focuses on aspirations, the Future Planning Workshop is a more pragmatic exercise, designed to transform these dreams into actionable plans. Here, partners come together to discuss the logistics of their shared future. Topics can range from financial planning, career trajectories, family planning, to decisions about where to live. It's a comprehensive session, grounded in realism, yet fueled by the dreams and aspirations identified in the dream board exercise. The goal is to emerge with a clear roadmap for the future, dotted with milestones, and infused with shared dreams and individual aspirations.

Building a shared future is akin to crafting a masterpiece. It requires patience, understanding, and a generous sprinkling of love. It's about celebrating the confluence of two paths while ensuring each retains its unique essence. It's about dreaming together, planning together, and walking hand in hand towards a horizon painted with shared hues of hope, love, and mutual respect. The journey might be fraught with challenges, differences, and occasional detours, but with a clear vision, unwavering support, and a heart full of love, the destination promises a future where dreams converge, and love reigns supreme.

Touchpoint 10. Keeping the Spark Alive

In the intricate waltz of relationships, there is an unspoken reality that the initial intensity, the passionate ardor, the unbridled enthusiasm might wane over time. It's not that the love diminishes, but as days morph into years and years into decades, the effervescence of initial courtship often settles into the calm familiarity of companionship. However, the essence of a flourishing relationship lies in nurturing this initial spark, in constantly rekindling the flame, ensuring it burns bright even amidst the mundanity of everyday life. Keeping the spark alive is more than just an effort; it's a testament to the commitment and the cherished value of the bond shared.

As love matures, so does its expression. The spontaneous adventures give way to planned vacations, late-night conversations become breakfast chats, and surprises are often limited to birthdays and anniversaries. But isn't love, in its most elemental form, about creating the unexpected? About breaking routines, rediscovering each other, and re-experiencing the moments that once made hearts race? It is these unexpected joys, the unpredictability, and the willingness to break the cycle of familiarity that instills freshness and keeps the heartbeats synchronized in excitement.

Maintaining excitement and passion in a relationship is akin to tending to a delicate plant. It requires regular care, a touch of creativity, and a profound understanding of the dynamics shared. Imagine a world where every day holds the potential for a surprise, where monotony is constantly challenged, and where the heart finds reasons to flutter with anticipation. In such a world, love doesn't just survive; it thrives, dances, and rejoices in its own existence.

Consider the exercise of a 'Surprise Day Out.' The premise is simple: once in a while, perhaps once a month or even once in a few months, one partner plans an entire day of activities without informing the other about the agenda. It could start with a surprise breakfast at a quaint cafe, a visit to a place both have never been before, or even a day of activities that one knows the other has always wanted to try. The beauty of this exercise lies in the unpredictability, in the joy of discovering the efforts taken, and in the shared experiences that ensue. It's a day where normal routines are disrupted, where cell phones might be ignored, and where the world outside fades into insignificance as the couple dives into a bubble of shared joy and surprises.

Then, there's the magic of nostalgia. Relationships are built on memories, on shared experiences, on moments that have been both challenging and joyous. Among these myriad memories, some stand out, glittering like stars in the vast expanse of shared time. One such memory, for most couples, is their first date – a day or evening filled with nervous anticipation, palpable excitement, and the thrill of the unknown. As time progresses, this memory often gets enveloped in the layers of numerous shared experiences, but its charm, its significance remains undiminished. The 'Recreate Your First Date' exercise is a beautiful dive into this memory. Couples are encouraged to relive that special day, to revisit the same places, wear similar outfits, and even have the same or similar conversations. It's not just about recreating the events, but about stirring the emotions that were felt, about re-experiencing the innocence, the nervousness, and the raw excitement of getting to know each other.

Both these exercises, while different in their approach, converge on a single premise – breaking the routine. They underscore the significance of unpredictability in a relationship, the importance of making efforts, and the joy of shared experiences. In relationships, it's often the little gestures, the unsaid words, and the unplanned adventures that create the most profound memories. It's the unexpected kiss, the unplanned drive, the surprise date, or the recreation of a cherished memory that reinforces the bond, reignites the passion, and reminds both partners of the reasons they chose each other in the first place.

Keeping the spark alive is not a task, not a checkbox in the relationship manual. It's an ongoing journey, a constant effort, a continuous dance. It's about waking up each day and choosing love, choosing excitement, choosing passion. It's about understanding that love, in its most genuine form, is not just about comfort and familiarity, but also about exploration, discovery, and constant reinvention. In the journey of love, every day can be an adventure, every moment a surprise, and every gesture a reaffirmation of the shared bond. All it requires is a willing heart, an eager soul, and the commitment to ensure that the spark, once ignited, never fades away.

Touchpoint 11. Reconnecting When Apart

Distance, in the context of relationships, often carries a somber undertone. Whether caused by career pursuits, personal quests, or unforeseen circumstances, the physical separation between loved ones can be a daunting challenge. Yet, as poets and philosophers have mused over centuries, love knows no boundaries. In the age of rapid technological advancement, the world has shrunk, and the miles have become mere numbers. But beyond technology, it's the strength of the bond, the intensity of the emotions, and the commitment to staying connected that keeps relationships alive, even when oceans apart.

Physical proximity undeniably adds a comforting dimension to relationships. The possibility of spontaneous meetings, impromptu dates, shared meals, and the warmth of a reassuring hug – these are luxuries that distance often snatches away. However, relationships aren't merely built on these physical interactions. They thrive on shared dreams, mutual respect, trust, and the unyielding bond of love. Distance, while challenging, can also be an opportunity, a litmus test of sorts, assessing the strength and depth of the bond shared.

The landscape of human connections has been transformed with the digital revolution. Today, lovers separated by vast distances can see each other at the click of a button, hear each other's voices anytime they wish, and even share experiences in real-time. But it's essential to recognize that while technology is a facilitator, the real connection happens in the heart, in the shared spaces of memories, dreams, and emotions.

Take the exercise of the 'Virtual Movie Night' for instance. The mechanics are simple. Both individuals choose a movie, ideally something they both love or are curious about. They then synchronize the start time, ensuring they are watching the movie simultaneously, even if they are time zones apart. As the film progresses, they can share reactions, discuss plot points, or simply enjoy the knowledge that somewhere, miles away, their loved one is sharing the same experience. It's a date night, redefined for the digital age. Yet, at its core, it's still two people, connected by love, sharing an experience, and creating a memory. It's about making an effort, finding a shared activity, and cherishing the virtual togetherness.

However, not all attempts to reconnect in the digital age need to be high-tech. There's a charm, a nostalgic beauty in embracing the old-world. This brings us to the 'Pen Pal Challenge.' The premise is delightfully old-fashioned. Both individuals commit to writing letters to each other, the old-fashioned way – with pen and paper. These letters are then posted and received in the tangible world, away from the instantaneity of the digital realm. The beauty of this exercise is manifold. Firstly, it brings back the charm of anticipation. The wait for a letter, the thrill of receiving it, and the joy of reading hand-written words is an experience that digital communication, for all its merits, can never replicate. Additionally, writing letters is an introspective journey. It forces one to slow down, to reflect, and to express emotions and thoughts with depth and sincerity. Over time, these letters become keepsakes, tangible memories of a time when distance was a part of the relationship's narrative.

Maintaining bonds in the face of distance is as much about these shared activities as it is about the mindset. It's crucial to view distance not as a roadblock but as a phase, a temporary detour in the larger journey of togetherness. Yes, there will be times of longing, moments of doubt, and periods of loneliness. Yet, with every virtual movie night and with every received letter, the distance diminishes, if not physically, then emotionally.

Relationships, in their most authentic form, are about mutual growth. And growth often comes from challenges. Distance, in this context, can be viewed as a challenge, but one that comes with its own set of rewards. It teaches patience, it instills trust, and it reinforces the belief that true love isn't about proximity but about connection. Whether it's through a synchronized movie experience or the joy of handwritten letters, the essence is to find ways, both modern and traditional, to bridge the gap, to fill the miles with memories, and to ensure that the heartstrings remain taut, resonating with the melodies of love.

Ultimately, the journey of love, even when punctuated by periods of distance, is about finding the harmony between the old and the new, the physical and the emotional, and the tangible and the intangible. It's about understanding that while love thrives in shared spaces and mutual experiences, its true strength is tested and often reinforced in the face of adversities. In the narrative of every relationship, distance can either be a poignant chapter or a transformative experience, and often, it's the efforts taken, the commitment shown, and the faith upheld that determines the story's trajectory.

Touchpoint 12. Groups

In the constellation of human connections, there's a mesmerizing allure in the bond between two individuals. Yet, as compelling as these intimate bonds are, there's a different magic altogether in group dynamics. When multiple individuals come together, bringing with them a medley of experiences, perspectives, and emotions, the resulting energy can be both challenging and transformative. Group touchpoints are about tapping into this energy, harnessing the collective power of multiple individuals to deepen bonds and build a resilient, empathetic community.

In a world where individual narratives often take precedence, the beauty of the collective sometimes gets overshadowed. However, history and anthropology provide countless examples of how communities, tribes, and collectives have been the backbone of human civilization. It's within groups that individuals find support, validation, shared joy, and collective strength during adversities. Modern urban living, with its fragmented lifestyle, may have disrupted traditional community structures, but the human yearning for belonging remains as potent as ever. Group touchpoints, in essence, are designed to rejuvenate this sense of belonging, to provide platforms where individuals can engage, relate, and grow together.

The 'Group Reflection Rounds' exercise is a powerful tool to facilitate deeper understanding and empathy within a group. The premise is simple but profound. The group gathers in a circle, a form symbolic of unity and equality. One by one, each member shares something - it could be a personal experience, a challenge they are currently facing, a memory that's dear to them, or even a dream or aspiration. The rule is that while one person speaks, the others listen with their full attention, without interruption or judgment. This active listening is crucial, for it's not just about hearing words, but about understanding emotions, recognizing vulnerabilities, and validating experiences. As each member shares, the group imbibes a bit of their story, their joys, their fears, and their dreams. Over time, this exercise transforms a group of individuals into a tapestry of shared stories, fostering understanding, empathy, and a deep sense of belonging.

Another remarkable exercise to harness the collective energy of a group is the 'Collaborative Touchpoint Projects.' At the heart of this exercise is the belief that creation, especially collaborative creation, is a powerful medium for connection. The group embarks on a project, something that demands collaboration, coordination, and collective decision-making. It could be as simple as creating a piece of art, organizing a community event, or even initiating a social responsibility project. The nature of the project isn't as crucial as the process of collaboration. As members brainstorm, delegate, take responsibility, and work together, they navigate the nuances of group dynamics. There are moments of agreement and instances of disagreements. There are times when the group's collective vision takes precedence, and times when individual expertise is celebrated. The journey, punctuated with challenges and triumphs, becomes a metaphor for the larger journey of life, where collaboration, understanding, and mutual respect pave the way for collective success.

Building community and deepening bonds in group settings require both vulnerability and strength. It's about celebrating the individual and the collective, recognizing that while every individual brings a unique flavor to the group, it's the collective energy that binds them together. It's about understanding that in the dance of group dynamics, every individual plays a role, whether as a leader, a supporter, a visionary, or a doer. It's about ensuring that every voice is heard, every perspective is considered, and every member feels valued.

Group touchpoints, as a concept, go beyond mere exercises. They are a philosophy, an acknowledgment of the human need for belonging, for being a part of something larger than oneself. In a world where individual success is often glorified, group touchpoints are a gentle reminder of the strength of the collective, of the magic that happens when individuals come together, with open hearts and open minds, to share, to collaborate, and to grow.

While the journey of every group is unique, shaped by the individuals within and the circumstances around, the essence remains universal. It's about finding common ground amidst diversity, about building bridges of understanding and empathy, and about harnessing the collective power to create, to celebrate, and to support. Whether it's through reflective sharing or collaborative projects, the goal is the same – to deepen bonds, to foster a sense of belonging, and to build a community where every individual, with their stories, dreams, and vulnerabilities, finds a space to call their own. It's a journey of coming together, of weaving individual narratives into a shared story, and of recognizing that in the dance of life, the solo performances are enchanting, but it's the group symphonies that resonate with the timeless melodies of connection, collaboration, and community.

Evolving Through Touchpoints

There's a gentle rhythm to life, a cyclical dance of change that plays out across our days, our months, our years. Relationships, too, move to this beat. But while nature has its ways to adapt, evolve, and bloom with each changing season, relationships require conscious effort. The vitality of a bond isn't a given; it's nurtured. And one of the most powerful ways to infuse this nourishment is through regular touchpoints — deliberate moments of connection, reflection, and growth.

Relationships are living entities, pulsating with the energies of two individuals. Just as a plant requires sunlight, water, and care, relationships thrive on understanding, communication, and regular check-ins. These aren't mere conversations but intentional touchpoints — moments when both parties pause, reflect, and deeply connect, aiming not just to sustain the relationship but to elevate it. In our busy lives, it's easy to lose sight of the 'us' amidst the whirlwind of individual routines. Days become weeks, weeks become months, and before we realize, we might feel we're drifting apart. But regular touchpoints act as anchors, grounding the relationship amidst the chaos, ensuring that the bond not just survives, but thrives.

One of the most potent tools to ensure the health and vitality of a relationship is the 'Monthly Relationship Touchpoint Review.' Imagine setting aside a dedicated evening every month, free from the distractions of work, chores, or digital devices. This is a sacred space for both of you, a moment in time reserved solely for the relationship. Begin by celebrating the highs, the shared joys, and the victories, no matter how small. Then, with an open heart and a non-judgmental mind, delve into the challenges, the hiccups, the misunderstandings. This isn't a space for blame but for understanding, a platform to express and to listen. By reviewing the month gone by, you're not just revisiting events but understanding patterns, recognizing triggers, and appreciating the growth. Over time, these monthly reviews become a cherished ritual, a touchpoint that both parties look forward to, a space that fosters connection, understanding, and mutual growth.

While the monthly reviews offer frequent touchpoints, ensuring the health of the relationship, there's a different energy to the 'Yearly Touchpoint Retreats.' Think of it as a relationship vacation, a break from the mundane, a time to celebrate each other. Choose a setting that resonates with both of you. It could be a secluded beach, a cabin in the woods, or even a cozy staycation at home. The essence is to create a bubble, a world where it's just the two of you, devoid of external distractions. This retreat is an opportunity to reflect on the year gone by, to celebrate the milestones, and to dream of the future. It's a space to reignite the spark, to rediscover each other, and to set intentions for the coming year. Engage in activities that bring you closer — it could be cooking a meal together, dancing under the stars, or simply cuddling up with a book. The goal is to connect, deeply and profoundly. And as you bid adieu to this retreat, you take back memories, renewed energy, and a deeper commitment to each other.

The beauty of touchpoints lies in their simplicity. They aren't grand gestures but sincere efforts, aimed at understanding, growing, and evolving together. They acknowledge that relationships, as living entities, require care and nourishment. They understand that while love is the foundation, it's the conscious efforts, the regular check-ins, and the shared dreams that build a relationship that's resilient, fulfilling, and ever-evolving.

As days turn into months and months into years, relationships, too, move through phases. There are days of sunshine, filled with laughter and shared dreams. And there are days of rain, punctuated with challenges and disagreements.

But through the sun and the rain, it's the touchpoints that act as the guiding stars, ensuring that the relationship remains on its growth trajectory. They are the moments when two individuals come together, leaving behind the weight of the world, to celebrate, to reflect, to dream. They are the moments that recognize that in the journey of love, it's not just about walking side by side but evolving, growing, and blossoming together.

By embedding touchpoints into the fabric of a relationship, one ensures that the bond remains fresh, vibrant, and alive. The monthly reviews act as gentle reminders, nudging the relationship back on track, ensuring that the bond remains strong and resilient. The yearly retreats, on the other hand, are a celebration, a time to rejoice in the magic of togetherness, and to set forth into another year with dreams in the eyes and love in the heart.

Relationships, at their core, are about two individuals coming together, bringing with them their dreams, their fears, their vulnerabilities. But through the journey, amidst the highs and the lows, it's the touchpoints that act as the glue, binding the individuals together, ensuring that the 'us' remains vibrant, alive, and ever-evolving. In the dance of love, touchpoints are the rhythm, the beat that ensures that both partners move in sync, celebrating the past, cherishing the present, and dreaming of a future filled with love, understanding, and togetherness.

Conclusion

In every symphony of life, there are melodies that stand out, resonating with the deepest chords of our hearts. In the grand composition of relationships, regular touchpoints and intimate check-ins are those harmonious notes. They're not just fleeting moments, but powerful heartbeats that ensure the living entity of a relationship remains vibrant, nurtured, and cherished. They bridge the spaces between two souls, ensuring that even in the cacophony of life, the song of love continues to play.

The lifelong journey of relationships is filled with myriad emotions. There are days of boundless joy, where love feels like an exhilarating dance. Then there are moments of introspection, where silence speaks louder than words. Yet, amidst these oscillations, regular touchpoints serve as guiding beacons. They aren't mere interruptions in the routine but are profound moments of connection. These are instances when two individuals, bound by love, pause to genuinely see each other, to understand, to empathize, and to grow. They ensure that the relationship, much like a well-tended garden, continues to bloom, season after season.

Consider the concept of touchpoints. They are not mandated timeouts or structured breaks. Instead, they are heart-centered pauses, moments when both individuals come together in genuine sincerity, leaving behind the masks they wear for the world. These are moments of vulnerability, of raw emotion, where words hold power, and silences echo understanding. They are platforms of validation, where each individual feels seen, heard, and valued. By embracing these touchpoints, couples ensure that the relationship remains anchored, even in the stormiest of times. They act as a compass, always pointing towards understanding, love, and togetherness.

Intimate check-ins, on the other hand, are deeper dives into the soul of the relationship. They're not casual conversations but profound heart-to-heart sessions. These check-ins are touchpoints magnified, moments when both parties explore the depths of their bond. They're platforms to celebrate the joys and navigate the challenges. They understand that every relationship has its rhythms, its unique dance. And these check-ins ensure that both partners remain in sync, moving gracefully through the stages of love. They act as mirrors, reflecting the true essence of the bond, ensuring that the relationship remains authentic, sincere, and genuine.

Embracing the rhythms of relationship touchpoints is akin to tuning into the most harmonious song of the heart. Every relationship has its tempo, its unique beat. And touchpoints, with their sincerity and depth, ensure that this rhythm remains alive and vibrant. They recognize that relationships aren't about grand gestures or dramatic declarations. Instead, they're about those little moments, those sincere pauses, those heart-centered touchpoints that breathe life into the bond. They're about understanding the silences, celebrating the words, and cherishing the shared dreams.

Imagine a world where every relationship, be it between partners, friends, or family, is punctuated with regular touchpoints. A world where individuals take a moment, amidst the hustle and bustle of life, to genuinely connect, to understand, and to grow together. Such a world would be filled with relationships that are not just sustained but cherished. Bonds that are not just maintained but nurtured. And love that is not just felt but lived.

In the end, the journey of relationships is a dance, a graceful waltz through the corridors of time. And touchpoints, with their depth, sincerity, and love, ensure that this dance remains beautiful, meaningful, and profound. They ensure that every step, every move, every twirl is in sync, resonating with the music of the heart. And as this dance continues, through the highs and the lows, it's the touchpoints that keep the magic alive, reminding every soul of the beauty, the wonder, and the miracle of love.

www.ingramcontent.com/pod-product-compliance
Lightning Source LLC
Chambersburg PA
CBHW071601270726
48661CB00017B/342